# ELI WHITNEY

## PEOPLE WHO MADE A DIFFERENCE

Ann Gaines

 Newbridge

A Haights Cross Communications Company

*Eli Whitney*
ISBN: 1-4007-3384-7

Published by
Newbridge Educational Publishing,
a Haights Cross Communications Company
333 East 38th Street, New York, NY 10016
*www.newbridgeonline.com*

Written by Ann Gaines

PHOTO CREDITS: Texas Department of Transportation, ©Archive Photos, Harper's
Weekly, Eli Whitney Museum

10 9 8 7 6 5 4 3 2 1

# TABLE OF CONTENTS

## ELI WHITNEY AND HIS INVENTION

Eli Whitney was an inventor. He made something no one had ever made before. In 1793, he made a machine to pull seeds out of freshly picked cotton. He called it a cotton gin. The name gin is another name for engine.

People use cotton to make cloth. Today most pants, shirts, and dresses are made with cotton.

*Cotton became the most important crop in the South.*

## A BOY WHO MADE USEFUL THINGS

Eli Whitney was born in Westboro, Massachusetts, on December 8, 1765. He was a boy who liked to make useful things. When he was a teen, he and his father built a **forge** in their barn. A forge is a special fireplace for heating metal.

Whitney learned to shape metal over the hot fire. He used the forge to make nails and hatpins to sell.

*Eli Whitney was born in this house.*

## THE PROBLEM WITH COTTON

After college, Eli Whitney moved to South Carolina. There he met Catherine Greene. She owned a large farm called a **plantation**.

She told him that cotton grew well on her land. Her problem was that cotton took too long to clean. One person working all day could pick the seeds out of just one pound of cotton. There had to be a better way!

*Workers pick cotton.*

Cotton is hard to clean because of its small black seeds. They hide inside a fluff of cotton, called a **cotton boll**. This cotton boll is the fruit of the cotton plant.

For thousands of years, people picked out seeds by hand. They pulled each seed along the cotton **fiber**, or thread. When the seed reached the end of the fiber, they tugged it off the cotton.

*Picking and taking the seeds out of cotton was a hard job.*

## THE COTTON GIN

Eli Whitney tried to think of a quicker way of getting seeds out of cotton. In his mind, he saw a machine with tiny wire fingers. The wire fingers picked the seeds from the cotton bolls.

Whitney remembered making things in the forge at home. He found scrap metal and wood at Catherine Greene's farm. Working quickly, he made a small cotton gin. He tried it and it worked!

*Whitney's cotton gin*

Eli Whitney knew Southern farmers would want to use his cotton gin. He also hoped to make money from it. He asked the government for a **patent**. He hoped his patent would protect his cotton gin from being copied by others.

He improved his machine. He received his patent in March of 1794.

*This drawing was used for the patent.*

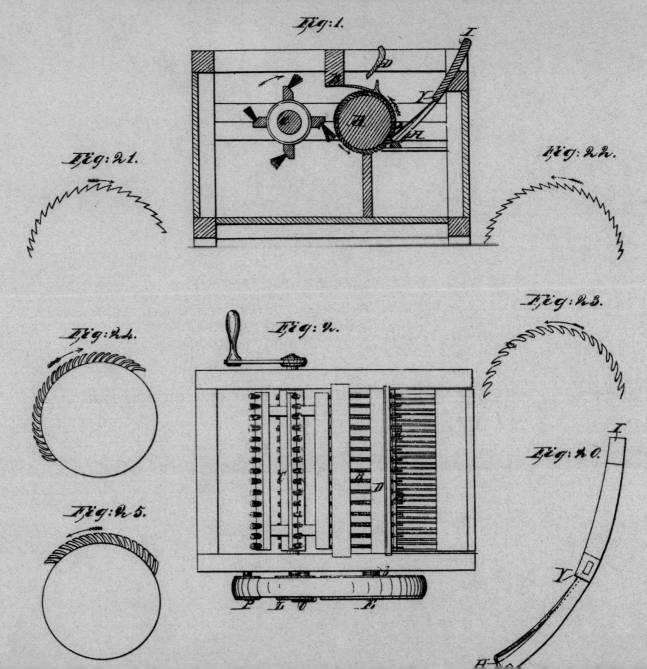

## MAKING COTTON GINS

Eli Whitney began building cotton gins. Many farmers used the new machines. They paid Whitney by giving him some of their cotton.

In 1795, Whitney's cotton gin factory burned down. Soon, farmers built their own cotton gins. They ignored Whitney's patent. They did not pay him for copying his machine. As a result, he never became rich from his invention.

*This cotton gin could clean seeds from 50 pounds of cotton a day.*

# ELI WHITNEY MAKES GUNS

In 1797, Eli Whitney invented machines to make gun parts. Workers put the parts together to make guns. Guns made by hand were all different. Whitney's guns were all the same. They were made quickly. They could also be quickly repaired.

The United States Army wanted more guns. They gave Whitney money to build a gun factory. He became the most important gun maker in the country.

*An old advertisement for Whitney's guns*

## REMEMBERING ELI WHITNEY

In 1817, Eli Whitney married Henrietta Edwards. They had four children. After a long sickness, he died January 8, 1825.

Farmers today use new cotton gins. The first cotton gin is on display in Washington, D.C., at the Smithsonian Museum of American History. People can also learn about him at the Eli Whitney Museum in Hamden, Connecticut.

*Today people use better machines for picking and cleaning cotton.*

## IMPORTANT DATES TO REMEMBER

| | |
|---|---|
| 1765 | Born in Westboro, Massachusetts (December 8) |
| 1794 | Received patent for cotton gin |
| 1795 | Cotton gin factory burned down |
| 1797 | Invented machines to make gun parts |
| 1817 | Married Henrietta Edwards |
| 1825 | Died after a long illness (January 8) |

# GLOSSARY

**cotton boll** (KAH ten BOWL) — the puffy white fruit of the cotton plant

**fiber** (FY ber) — a long, thin strand of material such as cotton or wool

**forge** (FORJ) — a workshop where fire is made hot enough so metal can be heated and formed into shape

**patent** (PAT nt) — a grant made by the government that says only the creator of an invention has the right to make, use, or sell the invention for a period of time

**plantation** (plan TAY shen) — a very large farm on which crops are raised

# INDEX

## Further Reading

Collins, Mary. *The Industrial Revolution*. Children's Press, 2000
Davies, Eryl. *Inventions.* Dorling Kindersley, 1995
Willing, Karen Bates. *Cotton*. Now and Then Publications, 1995

## Websites To Visit

www.yale.edu/ewhitney
www.nra.gov/education/cc/whitney.html

## About The Author

Ann Gaines is the author of many children's nonfiction books. She has also worked as a researcher in the American Civilization Program at the University of Texas.